Silver Dollar

by Jared Kelner

Title: Silver Dollar

Publisher: The Infinite Mind Training Group
(www.memory-trainers.com)

Playwright: Jared Kelner
(www.jaredkelner.com)

ISBN-13: 978-0-9826558-9-4
ISBN-10: 0982655894

All rights reserved. No part of this book may be reproduced or transmitted in any form or by any means without written permission from the playwright, except for the inclusion of brief quotations in a review.

Copyright © 2016 by Jared Kelner
All rights reserved.
First Edition, 2016

Published in the United States of America

Silver Dollar
by Jared Kelner

Written and Directed
by Jared Kelner

SILVER DOLLAR was produced by Fearless Productions and premiered at The Loft Theater at the Union County Performing Arts Center in Rahway, NJ on 4/8/2016, 4/9/2016 and 4/10/2016.

For Performance Inquiries Contact Jared Kelner at jared@jaredkelner.com

To watch a video of the original cast performance, please visit
www.jaredkelner.com/Pages/silverdollar.aspx

FEARLESS PRODUCTIONS

FEARLESS PRODUCTIONS (www.fearlessprod.com) strives to create entertaining theatrical productions that walk on the very edge of the edge, leap enthusiastically with our hearts on our sleeves, and dare to be daring. We recognize that the responsibility of true art is to firmly grasp the attention of our audience for as long as we are asking for it. We accept this challenge with the courage that only comes with doing exactly what we feel we were born to do... Simply put... Our NAME is our MISSION STATEMENT.

NOTES FROM THE PLAYWRIGHT

Secrets of abuse, buried for decades, are ripped to the surface and the truth leaves the family forever changed. After walking out on his fianceé and his family 18 years ago for reasons unknown, Donald returns home on the afternoon of his father's funeral, but why he's returned is not what it seems to be. SILVER DOLLAR has been described as an "incredibly uncomfortable drama...with substance and layers."

I hope that you leave this show transformed in some small way, that you have more questions than answers and that you give great thought to what might happen if the truths you once held to be sacred were shattered before your eyes.

Thank you to the many actors and friends that read the early drafts of SILVER DOLLAR and challenged me to dig deeper so I could discover each character's true voice and clarify their journey. I appreciate you all so very much.

Thank you FEARLESS PRODUCTIONS for the amazing support and generosity throughout this production.
I am humbled and honored to be connected with such a passionate and dedicated group of artists.

THE CAST

Jared Kelner as Donald

Brian Merrill as Lawrence

David Sussman as Wally

Kris Sussman as Katherine

Jared Kelner (Donald): Jared studied acting in NY, NJ and CA and has appeared professionally on Stage, TV and Film. Favorite roles include Ben/Malcolm in A PROMISE TO YOUR MOTHER, Alan in WHAT DO THEY BECOME?, Howard in RABBIT HOLE, George in GLENGARRY GLEN ROSS & Epstein in BILOXI BLUES. Jared recently appeared in the film MADELEINE directed by UK-Based Ollie Verschoyle. Jared is honored to have his third play brought to life by an incredible cast. Thank you Brian, David & Kristina for your commitment to this play. I am indebted to you all. Jared would like to thank his family for their love & support, and for giving him the opportunity to spend so much time in LaLa Land. A massive Thank You for the support from Brian Remo, Kristin Barber, Kara Wilson, Jessica Foerst, Katie Engle & the entire Fearless Productions family. Finally, Thank You to the UCPAC, the City of Rahway, Mayor Samson Steinman and his staff for their dedication to the arts and to their partnership with Fearless Productions. (jared@jaredkelner.com, www.jaredkelner.com)

Brian Merrill (Lawrence): Brian has been performing in plays and musicals for over 30 years. This is his first time working with Fearless

Productions. He would like to Thank Jared Kelner the writer, co-star, and director of Silver Dollar for trusting him with the complex role of Lawrence. He would also like to Thank Kristina, and David for their playful nature and professionalism. He would like to say Thank You to his friends and family, especially Bill, who continuously come out to support him.

David Sussman (Wally): Dave has been a Fearless member for just over two years, having started with the company in the Valentine's run of SRSL at the Producers club in NYC. Recently Dave took class with Jared and previously studied at McCarter Theater in Princeton and Just 3 of Us Studios in NYC. After starting in musical theater 34 years ago Dave had his eyes opened to "acting" in a production of Pippin under the direction of the late Ken Miller. There have been too many dramatic and comedic productions in Ocean and Monmouth counties and NYC to count. There have also been a number of commercial jobs and some indie movie roles, the latest being in Let Me Down Hard, which was just shown in the NJ Film Festival in A.C. Thanks to Jared, Brian, and my beautiful bride, Kris, for sharing the stage with me in this wonderful new work.

Kristina Sussman (Katherine): Kris is excited to make her stage debut with Fearless Productions, and is equally excited to be sharing the stage with her leading man, Dave. Thank you to her husband, Dave, to Jared Kelner and Brian Remo for encouraging her to fearlessly jump out of her comfort zone. Kris is thrilled to be a part of this amazing cast and is truly grateful to Jared for this opportunity to bring Katherine to life. Congratulations to the entire cast of Silver Dollar. Finally, a special Thanks to her kids for all their love and support.

CHARACTER DESCRIPTIONS

Walter (Wally) - Oldest Brother (~47)
Wally is damaged (physically, emotionally, psychologically), a child in a man's body, speaks with a speech impediment and like a child due to the brain trauma he suffered as a child

Donald (Donnie, Don) - Middle Brother (~46)
Donald is damaged, ashamed, angry, hurt, regretful, trying to make things right, aware of his flaws

Lawrence (Larry) - Youngest Brother (~45)
Lawrence is a caged animal, about to explode, at his wits end, exhausted, volatile, lost, hurt, abused

Katherine (Katie, Kate) – Lawrence's Wife, Donald's ex-Fianceé (~44)
Katherine is empty, abandoned, selfless to a fault, at the end of her rope, longing for love she'll never have, trying to survive one moment at a time, sad, a shell of her youthful self

Written and Directed
by Jared Kelner

Lights come up on the living room of Lawrence and Katherine's simple Westport, CT home. The room exudes lower-middle-class. The furniture is simple, older and worn. There is a feeling of tension and disarray in the haphazard arrangement of the furniture and items around the room. Center stage is a couch with 2 pillows, a rag quilt on the back, a small photo album on the cushion and end tables next to it on both sides. Behind the couch is a table with bottles of alcohol and glasses. Stage Right is a small dining room table with 2 chairs and 2 place settings. Stage left is the recliner (or larger chair) with a rag quilt on the back of the chair and a small child's knitted blanket on the seat, a small garbage can next to it on the floor and an end table to the stage left side. There are small flowers and cards on the end tables. Up-Stage Right is the front door to the house. Up-Stage Left is the corridor to the rest of the house where the bedrooms are presumed to be. It's 1pm, the day of Thomas Plunket's funeral. Tom, the father of the 3 brothers, owned a local business and warehouse. He was a towering presence of authority, masculinity and dominance. Tom died 3 days ago and as the play opens, Lawrence, Katherine and Wally are returning home after the funeral. As the lights come up full, Lawrence enters the room and takes in the silence. He is wearing traditional black funeral attire. He walks to the alcohol table behind the couch, puts his keys down, pours himself a bourbon straight-up and remains silently alone with his thoughts for a moment. From outside, we hear Wally and Katherine approaching. Wally and Katherine enter, both wearing traditional black funeral attire.

WALLY. (WALLY, holding his small bag full of quarters, speaks as they enter) Shiny quarters. Look at my shiny quarters, Kate. Hi, Lawrence, Look. Look. Look. Shiny quarters.

KATHERINE. Yes, Wally. So shiny. You love your quarters.

WALLY. I love my shiny quarters, Kate. Look. Look. Look. (KATHERINE reaches to look inside the small bag and WALLY slaps her hand away) You can't touch them. Let that be a lesson to you, Kate. My shiny quarters.

KATHERINE. Alright, Wally, I won't touch your quarters, but it is not nice to slap people, OK?

WALLY. OK, Kate. Sorry, Kate.

KATHERINE. It's OK, Wally. Come on, it's been a long day. Let's get you out of those clothes.

WALLY. Bath time.

KATHERINE. No, we are just going to change your clothes, Wally.

WALLY. Bath time. Wash the peepee.

KATHERINE. Wally, no. It is not bath time. And it is not nice to talk about your peepee.

WALLY. Wash the peepee, Kate.

KATHERINE. Lawrence, can you help me here?

LAWRENCE. Wally. Enough. Let Katherine change you.

WALLY. OK, Lawrence. Shiny quarters. Look. Look. Look. Shiny quarters Mommy gave me.
LAWRENCE. Hey! You know Dad's rule. We don't talk about that woman anymore, remember?
WALLY. I remember, Lawrence. Let that be a lesson to you.
LAWRENCE. Go get changed. You need to eat something. It's been a long day.
KATHERINE. Come on, Wally, let me take you upstairs.
WALLY. DADDY!! DADDY!! Where are you? You hiding?
KATHERINE. Wally.
WALLY. DADDY!!! Where are you? Look at my shiny quarters.
KATHERINE. Lawrence.
LAWRENCE. Wally. Enough!
WALLY. DADDY!!! You under the table? (WALLY picks up a knife from the table) Daddy, look, look, look. Shiny knife, Daddy.
LAWRENCE. Wally, put that down. You're going to hurt yourself.
WALLY. Shiny knife, Daddy.
LAWRENCE. Wally! Put it down. You're going to cut yourself.
WALLY. Owie, Lawrence, right?

LAWRENCE. Yes, Wally. It's sharp. The knife will give you an owie.

WALLY. Let that be a lesson to you, right, Lawrence?

LAWRENCE. Right, Wally.

WALLY. (WALLY puts the knife down) Daddy! Where are you hiding?

KATHERINE. Wally. Daddy died. Remember?

WALLY. Yeah, Daddy died. Where's he hiding?

LAWRENCE. He's not hiding, Wally.

WALLY. In the hole with the dirt and the big box. I saw him hiding.

LAWRENCE. Katherine, take him upstairs, please.

KATHERINE. I cannot do this now.

LAWRENCE. Kate, please.

KATHERINE. Wally, let's go change your clothes.

WALLY. Bath time. Wash the peepee.

KATHERINE. Lawrence!

LAWRENCE. Wally! Enough already!

KATHERINE. Wally, do you want to take a bath?

WALLY. Yeah.

KATHERINE. OK, let's get you into the bath.

WALLY. Wash the peepee.

LAWRENCE. Wally. Stop it. You do not talk to my wife like that.

WALLY. Donald's wife.

LAWRENCE. Katherine is my wife. She is not Donald's wife.
WALLY. (WALLY pinches KATHERINE'S breast) Quack, quack, like a duck. Donald's wife.
KATHERINE. Ow! That is not ok.
LAWRENCE. Wally!
WALLY. Quack, quack, like a duck. Donald's wife.
LAWRENCE. Get him out of here.
KATHERINE. Wally, you are not allowed to touch me like that.
WALLY. Shiny quarters. Look. Look. Look.
KATHERINE. Come on, Wally. Let's get you into the bath.
WALLY. Shiny quarters. Mommy gave me shiny quarters.
LAWRENCE. Wally! What did I say?
WALLY. I don't know.
KATHERINE. You want to wash your quarters? Make them real shiny?
WALLY. Yeah. Wash my quarters. Make them shiny.
KATHERINE. Good. Go upstairs. I will be right there.
WALLY. Kate. Guess what?
KATHERINE. It's bath time, Wally.
WALLY. Yeah, bath time, but you know what?
KATHERINE. What's that, Wally?

WALLY. I can say, "It's bath time" in Latin.

KATHERINE. In Latin?

WALLY. Yeah. I can say, "It's bath time" in Latin.

KATHERINE. You can?

WALLY. Yeah. Wanna hear?

KATHERINE. Sure, Wally.

WALLY. Yeah. A-it's...A-um...A-bath...A-time...A-in...A-Latin. Hahahahaha. I got you, Kate. Let that be a lesson to you, Kate.

KATHERINE. Very funny, Wally. That's pig-Latin, right?

WALLY. Yeah. Pig-Latin. Oink, oink like a pig-duck. Quack, quack like a duck, Kate. Quack, quack like a duck. Let that be a lesson to you, Kate.

KATHERINE. Wally, OK. Enough. It's bath time.

LAWRENCE. Wally! Take a bath already.

WALLY. Wash my quarters, Lawrence.

KATHERINE. Go upstairs and get out of your clothes, Wally. I'll start the bath for you in a minute.

WALLY. OK, Kate. Shiny quarters. Wash my quarters. (WALLY exits Up-Stage Left)

LAWRENCE. 38 years with those frigging quarters.

KATHERINE: (KATHERINE crosses to Lawrence) How are you?

LAWRENCE. I'm fine. Go take care of Wally.

KATHERINE. You buried your father today. You are not fine.

LAWRENCE. I'm fine.

KATHERINE. Do not shut me out.

LAWRENCE. Katherine, please. Let it be. I'm fine.

KATHERINE. OK...Was he there today?

LAWRENCE. Who?

KATHERINE. Who do you think?

LAWRENCE. How should I know? We haven't heard from him in 18 years.

WALLY. (Offstage) Kate. Bath time. Wash my quarters. I'm naked. Wash the peepee.

KATHERINE. (Calling up to WALLY) Just a minute, Wally. (Back to LAWRENCE) I didn't see him.

LAWRENCE. Then I guess he wasn't there.

KATHERINE. I looked for him.

LAWRENCE. Why would you do that?

KATHERINE. I thought he would be there.

LAWRENCE. And?

KATHERINE. And I did not see him.

LAWRENCE. Like the old man used to say, "Let that be a lesson to you."

KATHERINE. Don't be an ass.

LAWRENCE. I'm not the one looking for Donnie.

KATHERINE. He's your brother.

LAWRENCE. Brother? My brother's naked upstairs, waiting for you to wash his shiny quarters. That's the only brother I know.

KATHERINE. Stop being mean to me.

LAWRENCE. Well, don't go looking for ghosts.

KATHERINE. He's your brother, Lawrence.

LAWRENCE. I can't do this today, Katherine. We are not rehashing the same conversation.

KATHERINE. You have to stop blaming him.

LAWRENCE. Why are you pushing me?

KATHERINE. Because he is your brother.

LAWRENCE. He destroyed this family.

KATHERINE. Donald did not hit Wally on purpose. You know that.

LAWRENCE. He hit Wally in the head with a bat, Kate.

KATHERINE. I know the story, but it wasn't on purpose.

LAWRENCE. It ruined my mom.

KATHERINE. I know.

LAWRENCE. She left us.

KATHERINE. I know.

LAWRENCE. And he left you...on your wedding day.

KATHERINE. I remember.

LAWRENCE. So, let it go. Let him go. I don't get why you're pushing me on this.

KATHERINE. You have to forgive him.

LAWRENCE. Like you have?

KATHERINE. I am not talking about me, Lawrence. Your father died, your mother is...All I am saying is the only family you have left are your brothers.

LAWRENCE. Brother. We don't even know if he's is still alive.

KATHERINE. Donnie is alive.

LAWRENCE. Like it matters, Katherine? He's been gone 18 years. You didn't see him today. I didn't see him today. You know why? Because he's either dead or because he's a coward. A chicken-shit asshole that hit Wally in the head with a bat and destroyed this family. And your obsession to forgive him after what he did to you, I can't wrap my head around it. Look, I don't need this from you, especially today. Let me grieve. Let me breathe. Stop shoving Donnie down my throat.

WALLY. (Offstage) Kate. Bath time.

KATHERINE. (Calling up to WALLY) I'm coming, Wally. (Back to LAWRENCE) Finish your drink and when I get back down, this thing you're doing, better be done. I am not your punching bag and you will not lash out at me, not after everything I have sacrificed for this family. I do not deserve it and I will not tolerate it.

(KATHERINE grabs the cellphone out of LAWRENCE'S hands) Do you understand me, Lawrence? Do you understand me?

LAWRENCE. Give it to me.

KATHERINE. Do you understand me?

LAWRENCE. Yes.

KATHERINE. Good. (KATHERINE slams the cellphone on the table and exits Up-Stage Left. LAWRENCE refills his glass and sits down on the couch and begins to flip through a photo album. There's a knock at the front door. LAWRENCE calls up to KATHERINE)

LAWRENCE. I thought I told you to tell everyone we didn't want company.

KATHERINE. (Offstage) WHAT?

LAWRENCE. Nothing. (LAWRENCES crosses to the door Stage-Right and opens it. Standing there is DONALD in a Dark Jeans, a Long Sleeve Shirt and an Old Brown Leather Jacket)

DONALD. Larry.

LAWRENCE. You've got to be fucking kidding me.

DOLAND. The door was unlocked.

LAWRENCE. What do you want?

DONALD. Can I come in?

LAWRENCE. Why?

DONALD. Come on, Larry.

LAWRENCE. There's no money, Donald.

DONALD. I don't want his money.

LAWRENCE. Good. You're not getting the business, either. You're not getting nothing.

DONALD. I don't want anything from you.

LAWRENCE. Then what are you doing here?

DONALD. He died.

LAWRENCE. Yeah, I was there.

DONALD. So was I.

LAWRENCE. You were there?

DONALD. Yeah.

LAWRENCE. Where?

DONALD. In the back.

LAWRENCE. In the back? Like a coward.

DONALD. Whatever you need to tell yourself. Can I come in?

LAWRENCE. No.

DONALD. You think this is easy for me?...Larry, come on.

LAWRENCE. Fine. But I'm serious, Donnie. You're not getting anything.

DONALD. I don't want anything from you.

LAWRENCE. Because you left. You walked out on this family.

DONALD. I know that.

LAWRENCE. I'm staring at a ghost.

DONALD. I'm right here, Brother.

LAWRENCE. I can see that, but why? What for? Why are you here, Donnie?

DONALD. Burying my past, I guess.

LAWRENCE. Selfish.

DONALD. I don't see it like that.

LAWRENCE. You don't?

DONALD. No.

LAWRENCE. And?

DONALD. And, what?

LAWRENCE. Well you were there, today. He was buried. You saw that, from the back.

DONALD. Yes.

LAWRENCE. So, what are you still doing here?

DONALD. What do you mean?

LAWRENCE. Well, your past got buried today. I don't understand why you're still here.

DONALD. You want me to go?

LAWRENCE. I want to know why you're here. I want to know why you left without saying a word. I want to know where you've been. I want to understand how you just up and left Katherine and Wally and Dad and me with nothing. No note. No goodbye. No nothing. 18 years you're gone.

DONALD. I know that.

LAWRENCE. 18 years, Donnie. I thought you were dead. I thought you OD'd or something. I thought you got stabbed or shot or worse. I buried you in my mind many times, Donnie. Many times.

DONALD. I'm sorry.

LAWRENCE. I bet you are. I bet you're real sorry.

DONALD. This was a mistake.

LAWRENCE. You think?

DONALD. I'm gonna go.

LAWRENCE. Good.

DONALD. It was good to see you, Brother.

LAWRENCE. Get out of here.

DONALD. Tell Wally...

LAWRENCE. GET OUT OF HERE!!!

DONALD. OK, Larry. OK.

KATHERINE. (Speaking as she enters) Lawrence, what are you screaming at? (Pause) Donnie.

DONALD. Katie.

KATHERINE. You came.

DONALD. Yeah. You look...

LAWRENCE. No. You do not get to do that. That is my wife.

DONALD. You married him?

LAWRENCE. Get out!

DONALD. I want to see Wally.

LAWRENCE. No way.

DONALD. He's my brother.

LAWRENCE. Brother? You're no brother to us.

DONALD. Where is he?

LAWRENCE. You better get out of here, Donnie

DONALD. Or what?

KATHERINE. Stop it. The both of you. Please. Not today. Not now.

LAWRENCE. He's not staying here, Katherine.

KATHERINE. Lawrence, take a breath. Please. Calm down.

LAWRENCE. He does not get to just walk in here after 18 years and start making demands and calling you Katie.

DONALD. I want to see Wally.

LAWRENCE. I don't give a fuck what you want, Donnie. Get out of here.

DONALD. No

LAWRENCE. You're a child. You know that?

KATHERINE. Lawrence, please.

LAWRENCE. Don't get sucked in here, Katherine. He left. Remember that. He walked out on you. He left you standing up there alone like a fool.

KATHERINE. Watch yourself, Lawrence.

LAWRENCE. He left. I stayed. Remember that.

KATHERINE. Lawrence, take Wally out of the bath. Get him dressed and bring him down to see his brother.

LAWRENCE. And what? I'm supposed to leave you here, alone, with him? I don't think so.

KATHERINE. Lawrence, I am trying to hold it together here. I do not need you questioning my intensions. Get Wally dressed and bring him down.

LAWRENCE. Don't let him touch you. You hear me.

KATHERINE. Go.

LAWRENCE. Don't you fucking touch my wife.

(LAWRENCE exits Up-Stage Left)

DONALD. You married him?

KATHERINE. You left.

DONALD. How could you marry him?

KATHERINE. I don't need to explain myself to you, Donnie.

DONALD. But why did you stay?

KATHERINE. He was there. You left. He was there.

DONALD. But why didn't you leave? You didn't have to stay.

KATHERINE. Who else was going to take care of Wally? Lawrence? Your father? What choice did I have?

DONALD. You could've walked away.

KATHERINE. Like you did?

DONALD. (Pause) Any kids?

KATHERINE. No, Donnie. No kids.

DONALD. You should've walked away.

KATHERINE. He called me Katherine.

DONALD. Larry?

KATHERINE. No, Wally. He called me Katherine.

DONALD. What?

KATHERINE. He never called me Katherine. Always, Kate. Never Katherine. You left. Wally found me sitting alone outside the church. He sat down next to me and said, "Bye, bye, Donald. Smile, Katherine. Wally's here." So I stayed, Donnie. I stayed and Lawrence was there.

DONALD. I'm sorry.

KATHERINE. You're sorry? 18 years. Where did you go?

DONALD. You look good, Katie.

KATHERINE. Don't do that. Please. Stay over there.

DONALD. I'm sorry.

KATHERINE. Where did you go, Donnie? What happened to you?

DONALD. The funeral was nice. All the guys from the warehouse. I saw Crooked Charlie. I can't believe that guy's still alive. All twisted up like that. He must be like 85 or something.

KATHERINE. 87.

DONALD. No shit? 87. Amazing…Katie.

KATHERINE. Well?

DONALD. Can I get something to drink?

KATHERINE. The bar is right there. Help yourself.

DONALD. Just a glass of water. I don't drink anymore.

KATHERINE. I'm going to the kitchen to get you water.

DONALD. Thank you.

KATHERINE. I will be gone for one minute.

DONALD. OK.

KATHERINE. Will you still be here when I return?

DONALD. Katie, come on.

KATHERINE. Don't "Katie" me. You disappeared from my life and shattered my soul, so answer me. If I walk out of this room, will you still be here when I get back?

DONALD. Yes.

KATHERINE. Then sit down and don't move. Sit down, Donnie.

DONALD. (DONALD sits on the couch. KATHERINE exits to the kitchen. While KATHERINE is out of the room, DONALD looks at the pictures in the photo album on the coffee table. He sees a picture of his father) Hey, Dad. Looks like you're dead now.

Maybe you should've backed off the bourbon and the...well, you know what else, Daddy, right? Let that be a lesson to you. (KATHERINE enters with a glass of water. She hands it to DONALD and then steps away)

KATHERINE. Do you need ice?

DONALD. No, this is good. Thank you.

KATHERINE. You're looking through pictures?

DONALD. Yeah. Any of me in here?

KATHERINE. A few.

DONALD. Not a lot?

KATHERINE. Not as many as there should be. Lawrence burned most of them.

DONALD. Did he?

KATHERINE. Yes, but I put a few back in.

DONALD. You did?

KATHERINE. For Wally.

DONALD. Not for you?

KATHERINE. For Wally.

DONALD. For Wally. How is he?

KATHERINE. Donnie.

DONALD. Yeah?

KATHERINE. Why did you leave me?

DONALD. (DONALD gets up and crosses to the table) Katherine, I... (LAWRENCE and WALLY enter)

Wally! (DONALD and WALLY slowly cross to the center and embrace)

WALLY. (WALLY pinches DONALD'S breast) Quack, quack, like a duck, Donald.

DONALD. (DONALD pinches WALLY'S breast) Quack, quack, like a duck, Wally.

WALLY. Your face has lines on it, Donald.

DONALD. I got old, Buddy.

WALLY. Yeah, you got old, Buddy. Your hair is gone.

DONALD. Yes, it is.

WALLY. Why did you cut off your hair, Donald?

DONALD. It fell out, Wally.

WALLY. Why did it fall out, Donald? Are you old now?

DONALD. Maybe a little bit old, Wally.

WALLY. Not old like Daddy. Cause Daddy died, Donald. Daddy died.

DONALD. I know, Wally. I was at the funeral.

WALLY. You saw Daddy hiding in the box in the dirt?

DONALD. I saw him, Wally.

WALLY. Where's Daddy hiding now, Donald?

DONALD. Wally, Daddy's not hiding. Daddy died.

WALLY. Yeah. Daddy died. He's dead now...Donald?

DONALD. Yeah, Wally?

WALLY. Why you don't sleep in this house anymore?

LAWRENCE. Yeah, Donald, "why you don't sleep in this house anymore?"
WALLY. You sleep at another house now?
DONALD. Yes, Wally. I sleep at another house now.
WALLY. Why, Donald? You don't love me anymore?
DONALD. Hey, Buddy, of course I still love you. I will always love you. You're my brother.
WALLY. You don't love Lawrence anymore?
DONALD. I still love Lawrence.
LAWRENCE. Like hell you do.
WALLY. You don't love Kate anymore?
LAWRENCE. Careful, Donald.
DONALD. I love all of you, very much.
WALLY. And Mommy? You still love Mommy, Donald?
LAWRENCE. Wally, what did Dad say about not talking about her?
DONALD. He can talk about her if he wants to.
LAWRENCE. Like hell he can.
DONALD. What's your problem?
WALLY. Daddy, too? You still love Daddy, Donald?
DONALD. Look, Wally, it's complicated.
WALLY. But you still love Daddy, Donald, right? Cause Daddy died, Donald, Daddy died in a box in the dirt. I saw him hiding.

KATHERINE. Yes, Wally, we buried Daddy today, but we can go visit him whenever you want. Would you like that?

WALLY. Yeah. I'm gonna visit Daddy in the box.

KATHERINE. And we can bring him flowers, too, Wally. Wouldn't that be a nice thing to do?

WALLY. Yeah. But no flowers, Kate, cause Daddy was a bad boy.

KATHERINE. Why is Daddy a bad boy, Wally?

WALLY. Daddy died cause he was a bad boy. Let that be a lesson to you.

DONALD. What?

WALLY. Let that be a lesson to you.

DONALD. Why would you say that?

WALLY. Daddy died because he was a bad boy. He got punished bad, so God made him get dead in a box.

KATHERINE. Wally, Daddy did not die because he was a bad boy. He died because he was sick.

DONALD. You got that right, Kate. He was sick. Sick in the fucking head.

LAWRENCE. Hey! Watch it.

DONALD. He was a sick fuck, Larry.

LAWRENCE. What is your problem? The man's body is still warm. Show some respect.

DONALD. For that monster? Never.

LAWRENCE. Why are you here? What are you doing here? You need money, don't you? How much to make you go away again, Donnie? Come on. Name your price. I'll pay it. I'll pay it, cash money, right now.
KATHERINE. Lawrence, please stop. Not in front of Wally.
WALLY. Donald, look at my shiny quarters.
LAWRENCE. Not now, Wally.
WALLY. Donald, look at my shiny quarters.
LAWRENCE. I said not now, Wally. (LAWRENCE shoves WALLY)
KATHERINE. HEY!
DONALD. Back off, Larry. Wally wants me to see his quarters.
WALLY. Donald, look at my shiny quarters. Mommy gave me shiny quarters.
DONALD. She did?
WALLY. Yeah. I washed them in the bath. Make them shiny. Clean off all the dirt.
DONALD. Did you?
WALLY. Yeah. I washed my shiny quarters in the bath. Wash the peepee in the bath.
KATHERINE. Wally, I told you not to say that.
WALLY. Let that be a lesson to you. Wash the peepee.
LAWRENCE. Wally, stop it!

DONALD. Shut up, Larry. Wally? Who said that to you?
WALLY. Wash the peepee. Let that be a lesson to you.
DONALD. Who said that, Wally?
WALLY. Daddy died, Donald.
DONALD. I know that, Wally.
WALLY. He was a bad boy.
DONALD. Who was a bad boy?
WALLY. Wally.
DONALD. Wally was a bad boy?
WALLY. Yeah.
DONALD. And what happens to bad boys?
WALLY. Wash the peepee.
LAWRENCE. What is he talking about?
DONALD. What happens to bad boys?
WALLY. I don't know.
DONALD. What did Daddy make bad boys do?
LAWRENCE. What are you doing, Donald?
DONALD. Shut up, Larry! Wally. Look at me.
WALLY. I see you. You have lines on your face.
DONALD. What happens to bad boys?
WALLY. I don't know.
DONALD. What did Daddy make bad boys do?
WALLY. Wash the peepee.
DONALD. Who's peepee, Wally?
KATHERINE. Oh, my God.

DONALD. Who's peepee, Wally?

WALLY. Daddy's peepee.

LAWRENCE. What is this?

DONALD. Shut up, Larry.

KATHERINE. Please, God, no.

DONALD. Were you a bad boy, Wally?

WALLY. Yeah.

DONALD. Why, Wally? What did you do bad?

WALLY. Sissy girl.

DONALD. You ran like a girl?

WALLY. Pansy girl.

DONALD. Who told you that, Wally? Who called you names?

WALLY. Daddy.

DONALD. And that made you a bad boy?

WALLY. Yeah. Wally is a sissy girl.

KATHERINE. No, you're not, Wally. You're a good boy.

WALLY. I'm a bad boy. Wash the peepee. Let that be a lesson to you.

LAWRENCE. What is he talking about, Katherine?

DONALD. Wally, can I see your quarters?

WALLY. Look, Donald. My shiny quarters.

DONALD. Wow, Wally. They are so shiny. I bet if you sit down at the table and play with your quarters you can stack them really high. Make a big tower.

WALLY. Stack my shiny quarters.

DONALD. Yeah. Come sit down at the table and stack your quarters.

LAWRENCE. What the fuck is going on here?

DONALD. (DONALD helps WALLY to the table) Larry, I think you should sit down.

LAWRENCE. Fuck that. What is he talking about, Katherine?

KATHERINE. I don't know.

DONALD. The story.

LAWRENCE. What story?

DONALD. The story of Wally and the bat.

LAWRENCE. I know the story, Don. Dad told it a hundred times. You know the story too, right Katherine?

KATHERINE. I know the story, Lawrence. (KATHERINE gets up from the arm of the couch, crosses behind the couch and sits at the table next to WALLY)

LAWRENCE. See, Donnie. You know the story. I know the story. Katie here, she knows the story, too. I mean I haven't heard it in, what's it been, 18 years, but I remember it well. Dad and you and Wally were out playing baseball while mom and I were getting me clothes. Dad pitched. Wally was catching. You swung and missed and the ball hit you in the eye, but you,

standing so far back cause you were a scared little boy, weren't you, you hit Wally in the back of the head with the bat and knocked him out. Then you ran away like the chicken shit you are and left your brother with a cracked skull bleeding on the ground. I know the story, Don. I know it well.
DONALD. That's not what happened.
LAWRENCE. What do you mean, "That's not what happened"? That's what happened, Donald. That's the story. That's how it goes.
DONALD. You weren't there, Larry.
LAWRENCE. You rewriting history now, Donnie Boy? Cause you can't deal with the guilt?
DONALD. You weren't there and that's not what happened. That's what Dad said happened to protect his criminal ass, but none of it is true.
LAWRENCE. None of it's true?
DONALD. No.
LAWRENCE. Then what happened, Donnie? Why don't you enlighten us.
KATHERINE. Donnie?
DONALD. You were with mom, Larry. I think getting clothes like you said. I don't know that part, maybe that's true. I don't know. Dad took us out to play ball. I got up to bat. Wally was catching.

LAWRENCE. I already said that.

DONALD. Dad pitched and I hit the ball right back to him.

LAWRENCE. Bullshit.

DONALD. So, he pitched again. A little faster this time and I hit a shot down first.

LAWRENCE. That's not what happened.

DONALD. He made Wally run and get the ball. The whole time he was running, Dad kept screaming at him shit like, "Come on you sissy." "You run like a girl." "Lift those knees up, you pansy." Wally got the ball and threw it back to Dad, but Wally threw, kind of, ah fuck, kind of girly. So Dad rips into him again, grabbing him hard to make him throw like a man. Wally started crying. I was screaming at Dad to let him go, but he didn't stop. So, I picked up the bat and swung it.

LAWRENCE. And you it Wally in the head.

DONALD. No, Larry. I hit Dad in his shin and he dropped to his knees. He was looking at me, eye to eye. I could smell the bourbon coming up from his gut. Then he shoved Wally to the ground and grabbed me by the shirt. He cocked his fist back and punched me in the eye, right where that baseball supposedly hit me. It was his fist, Lawrence. Not the ball.

LAWRENCE. This is such bullshit.

DONALD. Wally was crying. I got up from the grass and ran away. I should've stayed to protect Wally, but I ran, Lawrence. You're right. I was a chicken shit. I was scared shitless of Dad. I ran into the woods and I watched him get up and yank Wally by the hair. Dad was screaming at him and smacking him as he dragged Wally back to the car. "You're a bad boy, Wally." "You run like a sissy girl." "Let that be a lesson to you."

WALLY. Let that be a lesson to you.

DONALD. I ran home. When I got back, mom's car wasn't there. You were still out with her. I went inside. I heard Wally crying in the bathroom, so I opened the door. The shower was on. I reached out and pulled the curtain back.

LAWRENCE. And?

DONALD. And Wally was in there. Facing Dad. I looked up at this wrinkled, disgusting man. Dad had his head back and his eyes closed so he didn't see me. Wally stopped and Dad opened his eyes. And then...

KATHERINE. What?

DONALD. He lost it, Kate. He went mad. Like when Mom backed the truck into the mailbox. You remember that, Larry, right?

LAWRENCE. No.

DONALD. Well he did. He beat her ass, Larry. How do you not remember that?

LAWRENCE. Cause I don't, ok?

DONALD. Whatever. So, Dad opens his eyes cause Wally stopped and, like I said, he went mad. Dad shoved him so hard that Wally went flying back and cracked his head on the tile behind him. He dropped like he was dead and there was a lot of blood. Dad hauled back and punched me in the fucking eye again and knocked me to the ground. He lost it. I'm telling you the truth, Larry. He was cursing and screaming. He jumped out of the shower and grabbed a towel and yanked Wally from the tub. He kept screaming, "Let that be a lesson to you." "Let that be a lesson to you."

WALLY. Let that be a lesson to you.

DONALD. He carried Wally unconscious to our room and made me dry him off and put his dirty clothes back on him while Dad held a towel around his head so blood didn't get on the carpet. He looked at me and said, "If you tell anyone about any of this, I will murder you." And he meant it. So I shut my fucking mouth. He got dressed and ran out of the house carrying Wally, tossed him into the Chevy and drove to the hospital. He told everyone I hit Wally in the head with the bat. But that's not what happened, Larry. That's not what happened.

LAWRENCE. That is so convenient, Donnie.

DONALD. It's the truth.

LAWRENCE. Sure it is. It makes perfect sense that you come back now once Dad's dead to rewrite history. To clear your conscience cause you got demons keeping you up at night. Making him out to be some kind of monster. Why now, Donnie? Why come back now?

KATHERINE. You don't believe him?

LAWRENCE. No.

DONALD. Why would I lie about this?

LAWRENCE. Cause you're a loser.

KATHERINE. Lawrence! What is your problem?

LAWRENCE. Don't start in on me, Katherine.

DONALD. Back off, Larry.

LAWRENCE. Fuck you, Donnie. You come in here spouting lies. You expect me to believe you walked in on Wally sucking Dad off cause he was a bad boy.

DONALD. Yes.

LAWRENCE. You're full of shit, you coward.

DONALD. It's the truth.

LAWRENCE. Like hell it is.

DONALD. I'm telling the truth, Larry.

LAWRENCE. Bullshit.

DONALD. You just don't want to see it.
LAWRENCE. There's nothing to see cause it's all bullshit.
KATHERINE. How did you know, Lawrence?
LAWRENCE. Know what? What are you talking about?
KATHERINE. What Wally was doing to your father in the shower?
LAWRENCE. What? What are you talking about?
KATHERINE. You just said, "You expect me to believe you walked in on Wally...sucking Dad off...cause he was a bad boy."
LAWRENCE. Yeah? So what?
KATHERINE. How did you know what Wally was doing?
LAWRENCE. Cause Donnie just said it.
KATHERINE. No, he didn't.
LAWRENCE. Yes he did, Kate. He said he saw Wally on his knees in front of dad.
KATHERINE. No, he didn't, Lawrence.
LAWRENCE. Yes, he did.
DONALD. No, I didn't. I said I saw Wally facing Dad, but I never said he was on his knees.
LAWRENCE. What? So what? What's the difference?
DONALD. But he was.
LAWRENCE. What?

DONALD. On his knees. How did you know Wally was on his knees, Lawrence?
LAWRENCE. I don't know what you're talking about?
KATHERINE. Oh, my God.
DONALD. How did you know?
LAWRENCE. I didn't know shit. What the fuck is the matter with you people. Donnie is the liar here, Katherine, coming in and making up stories about a dead man.
DONALD. He did it to you, too.
LAWRENCE. Fuck you, Donald. No, he didn't.
WALLY. (WALLY leaves his quarters stacked up on the table, stands, and moves behind DONALD) Let that be a lesson to you, Lawrence.
LAWRENCE. Shut up, Wally.
KATHERINE. Lawrence.
LAWRENCE. Shut the fuck up.
DONALD. Larry, it's ok. It's not your fault. You didn't do anything wrong.
LAWRENCE. You better shut your fucking mouth you asshole or I will murder you.
KATHERINE. Calm down, Lawrence.
LAWRENCE. Shut up.
DONALD. Larry, you're not alone here.

LAWRENCE. AAAAAHHHHHH!!!!! (LAWRENCE lunges at DONALD and throws a punch. He misses and punches WALLY in the face. WALLY drops to the floor)

KATHERINE. LAWRENCE! (They all stand silently over WALLY)

WALLY. Owie! Owie! (WALLY jumps up and runs out of the house)

DONALD. WALLY!!!

LAWRENCE. WALLY!!! COME BACK!!! I'M SORRY!!! WALLY!!! (LAWRENCE runs out after WALLY)

DONALD. Should I go after him?

KATHERINE. No. He knows where Wally hides when he's scared. He'll bring Wally back.

DONALD. I didn't mean for that to happen, Katie.

KATHERINE. I know, Donnie.

DONALD. I need a drink.

KATHERINE. No, you don't.

DONALD. Yes, I do.

KATHERINE. Drink the water, Don.

DONALD. Yeah. Drink the water.

KATHERINE. Are you ok? Did he hurt you?

DONALD. No, he missed me. I'm ok. Maybe just sit down for a minute. (DONALD and KATHERINE sit down on the couch)

KATHERINE. Sure. Do you want to talk about it?

DONALD. I don't think so.

KATHERINE. OK. We can just sit here.

DONALD. Yeah. That'd be nice. Is Wally going to be alright?

KATHERINE. I think so.

DONALD. Good. I hope Larry didn't hurt him.

KATHERINE. Me, too...I missed you, Donnie. Every day. I missed you very much. Did you miss me?

DONALD. Katie.

KATHERINE. Did you think about me, Donnie?

DONALD. Of course.

KATHERINE. I don't understand. What happened? Why did you leave me? Did I do something wrong?

DONALD. No. God, no.

KATHERINE. Then what was it? Why would you break my heart like that?

DONALD. You said...

KATHERINE. What? What did I say?

DONALD. You said you wanted a son.

KATHERINE. What? When?

DONALD. The night before our wedding.

KATHERINE. What are you talking about?

DONALD. You said you wanted a son. You said you wanted to have a baby boy with me and name him Winston, after your father. Do you remember?

KATHERINE. Yes.

DONALD. We fought. It was a bad one. Do you remember that?

KATHERINE. Yes. You said you'd never name a child after a cigarette.

DONALD. And then I stormed out.

KATHERINE. That was last time I saw you.

DONALD. It wasn't about the name.

KATHERINE. No?

DONALD. No, Kate. It was about my Dad.

KATHERINE. What do you mean?

DONALD. There was no way I was going to bring a child into this family while that monster was still alive. I knew how much you wanted a baby. That's all you talked about and I was never going to let that happen, Kate. We would've fought, a lot. For years. And you would've grown bitter and resented me, hated me, for depriving you the chance to be a mom. But I couldn't let that man near my son, so I left. I left you to protect an unborn child and so you could live and find someone else. So you could have a baby and be a mom. I never thought even for one second that you would've stayed, Katie. You've got to believe me.

KATHERINE. (KATHERINE stands) That can't be why. I cannot allow that to be the reason you left me.

DONALD. It's the truth. I owe you that much.

KATHERINE. I was broken inside.

DONALD. I know that, Katie.

KATHERINE. No, Donald. My insides were broken.

DONALD. What?

KATHERINE. My insides didn't work like they were supposed to.

DONALD. What do you mean?

KATHERINE. My insides were broken. They were never going to make a baby no matter how hard we tried. So, they took out the broken pieces and left me empty inside. I was never going to be able to have your son, Donald. Ever.

DONALD. What?

KATHERINE. (KATHERINE steps backward to balance herself on the table behind her. As she supports herself, the stacks of quarters topple over onto the table) You didn't have to leave me.

DONALD. Katie. (KATHERINE runs out of the room to the kitchen leaving DONALD alone. DONALD sits down at the table and puts WALLY's quarters back the pouch. Moments later LAWRENCE and WALLY enter from the front door) Is he ok?

LAWRENCE. Wally's a good boy. He's strong. Isn't that right, Wally?

WALLY. Yeah.
LAWRENCE. Yes, you are, Wally. And I love you. You know that, right?
WALLY. Yeah.
LAWRENCE. That's a good boy, Wally. Why don't we get you cleaned up?
WALLY. OK, Lawrence.
LAWRENCE. Where's Katherine?
DONALD. In the kitchen.
LAWRENCE. Katherine. (KATHERINE enters but stands by the kitchen doorway) Would you help get Wally cleaned up? I'd like to talk to my brother.
KATHERINE. Of course. Wally, come here, Sweetie. Let's get you cleaned up and put something cold on that eye. (WALLY and KATHERINE exit into the kitchen leaving LAWRENCE and DONALD alone)
LAWRENCE. (LAWRENCE pours himself a drink and sits down on chair) What a day, huh?
DONALD. What a day. You ok?
LAWRENCE. We buried our father today.
DONALD. Yeah. Somehow, I never thought he was going to die.
LAWRENCE. Yeah. He was a crusty old man for a long time.
DONALD. He was old even when he was young.

LAWRENCE. Yes, he was.

DONALD. (DONALD, holding the pouch of quarters, stands and moves toward LAWRENCE) You know, Larry...

LAWRENCE. Look, Donnie. I don't want to talk about it, ok?

DONALD. Yeah, sure. OK. (DONALD sits down on the couch, puts the quarters on the couch next to him, picks up the photo album and flips through it aimlessly)

LAWRENCE. Thanks. I'm glad you're here.

DONALD. Me, too.

LAWRENCE. I missed you.

DONALD. Yeah.

LAWRENCE. Ah fuck, look at us, getting all pansy-ass with each other. Dad would've hated that.

DONALD. Fuck him, Lawrence.

LAWRENCE. Yes. Fuck him.

DONALD. Some funny pictures in here, huh, Lawrence?

LAWRENCE. I burned the ones of you.

DONALD. Yeah, Katie told me.

LAWRENCE. But she put some of you back in.

DONALD. Yeah, for Wally.

LAWRENCE. Whatever you have to tell yourself, Donnie.

DONALD. What?

LAWRENCE. Come on, man. I saw the way she looked at you.

DONALD. She was just surprised to see me. That's all.

LAWRENCE. That was not surprise on my wife's face, Donald. That was love.

DONALD. No. Come on, Lawrence. It's not like that. I've been gone a long time.

LAWRENCE. Like I said, whatever you have to tell yourself, Donnie.

DONALD. You got nothing to worry about. (Pointing to a picture in the photo album) Hey, here's Crooked Charlie. I saw him at the funeral. I can't believe that guy's still alive.

LAWRENCE. He's still kicking. 87 this year. We had this big party for him at the warehouse.

DONALD. Amazing. All twisted up like that. How does he do work?

LAWRENCE. (LAWRENCE pantomimes a crooked, twisted body moving) Like this.

DONALD. Dad told me once how Charlie got all crooked.

LAWRENCE. I know the story, but look, Don, I don't

want to talk about Dad right now.

DONALD. Yeah, of course. I'm sorry.

LAWRENCE. No, it's ok.

DONALD. Fuck.

LAWRENCE. Yeah, fuck.

DONALD. Lawrence.

LAWRENCE. What is it?

DONALD. I've got something to tell you.

LAWRENCE. More? You got more to tell me?

DONALD. Yeah.

LAWRENCE. I guess that's what happens when you don't talk for 18 years. OK. What do you got?

DONALD. I found her.

LAWRENCE. You found her?

DONALD. Yeah.

LAWRENCE. Found who?

DONALD. Mom.

LAWRENCE. (LAWRENCE stands and moves Stage Left) You've got to be fucking kidding me. I can't do this now. Not today, Donnie. Not today... She's alive?

DONALD. Yeah.

LAWRENCE. Where is she?

DONALD. She gave me something to give to you.

LAWRENCE. You saw her? You talked to her?

DONALD. Yeah.

LAWRENCE. When?

DONALD. Recently.

LAWRENCE. That just perfect. Where is she?

DONALD. Providence.

LAWRENCE. Rhode Island?

DONALD. Yeah.

LAWRENCE. Rhode-Fucking-Island?

DONALD. Yeah.

LAWRENCE. That's like 2 hours away, Donnie.

DONALD. Yeah.

LAWRENCE. She's been there the whole time?

DONALD. Yeah.

LAWRENCE. And what, you've seen her?

DONALD. I've been staying with her.

LAWRENCE. You're staying with her?

DONALD. Yeah.

LAWRENCE. Are you out of your fucking mind, Donnie? She abandoned us.

DONALD. I know.

LAWRENCE. What is she sick or something?

DONALD. Yeah.

LAWRENCE. She's sick?

DONALD. Yeah, Larry. She's sick.

LAWRENCE. Well, ain't that the cherry on top of the shit sundae.

DONALD. I'm sorry.

LAWRENCE. She's like sick, sick?

DONALD. I don't know, maybe. They don't know yet. They're running tests and shit, but she's old, Larry. You know. It's like, you get old and your body just starts to crumble inside.

LAWRENCE. (LAWRENCE moves to the alcohol table to refill his drink) So, that's why you're here. That's why you came back. To tell me you found mom.

DONALD. Yeah.

LAWRENCE. Not for the funeral?

DONALD. No, it just sort of worked out that way.

LAWRENCE. Would you have come?

DONALD. No, Lawrence. I would not have come.

LAWRENCE. OK, Donnie. OK.

DONALD. She asked me to give you something.

LAWRENCE. Me? (LAWRENCE moves Stage Right behind the couch)

DONALD. Yeah. (DONALD pulls out an envelope from his jacket pocket)

LAWRENCE. What is that?

DONALD. A letter.

LAWRENCE. Some apology note or something?

DONALD. I don't know. I didn't read it.

LAWRENCE. I don't want that.

DONALD. She made me promise I'd give it to you.
LAWRENCE. I don't care…What does it say?
DONALD. I didn't read it.
LAWRENCE. Yeah, well, I don't think I want to read it either.
DONALD. I get it. (DONALD puts the letter on the coffee table) Maybe if I just leave it here for you for when you're ready, you know, to read it. (DONALD picks up the pouch of quarters, stands and moves Stage Left)
LAWRENCE. Yeah. Maybe one day when I'm ready. (LAWRENCE stares at the letter and then grabs it and moves Down-Stage Right in front of the table). Ah, fuck this shit. (LAWRENCE opens the envelope and reads the letter silently to himself and is quite affected by what is written) Says here she knew what Dad did to us.
DONALD. Yes, she did.
LAWRENCE. Unbelievable. (LAWRENE continues reading the letter) Holy shit! Did you know about the quarters?
DONALD. She told me.
LAWRENCE. It was a pay off? Is that what they were? She gave him a quarter every time Dad that? Is she fucking kidding me? A quarter?

DONALD. It helped Wally forget.
LAWRENCE. Donnie, he's got a sack full of them.
DONALD. I know.
LAWRENCE. A sack-full, Donnie. What was she thinking? Fuck, I didn't get any quarters. Where are my quarters? Did she run out of pocket change or something? She didn't give me any fucking quarters, Donnie. Not a single one.
DONALD. She bought you clothes.
LAWRENCE. What?
DONALD. Clothes, Larry. She took you shopping for clothes. That was your quarters.
LAWRENCE. Bullshit.
DONALD. Think about it.
LAWRENCE. Fuck, me. And what about you? What were your quarters?
DONALD. Baseball cards.
LAWRENCE. There's a box of them in attic with your name on it.
DONALD. Yes, there is.
LAWRENCE. You want them?
DONALD. No.
LAWRENCE. (LAWRENCE puts the letter back in the envelope) Why didn't she take us with her, Donnie?
DONALD. She was scared.

LAWRENCE. Of what?

DONALD. Of him. He beat her, Larry. You don't remember that?

LAWRENCE. It was a long time ago.

DONALD. It happened. A lot.

LAWRENCE. She should've taken us with her. Get us all out. But no, she left us with him.

DONALD. Yes, she did.

LAWRENCE. Why would a mother do that, Donnie?

DONALD. (DONALD sits down on the couch) I don't know. But you can ask her.

LAWRENCE. What?

DONALD. She wants to see you.

LAWRENCE. What for?

DONALD. I guess to say she's sorry.

LAWRENCE. Is that what she told you?

DONALD. Yeah.

LAWRENCE. Why now?

DONALD. She's sick, Lawrence.

LAWRENCE. Right. She's sick.

DONALD. Yeah.

LAWRENCE. Providence, huh?

DONALD. Yeah, Providence.

LAWRENCE. Let me think on it. (LAWRENCE sits down at the table)

DONALD. Yeah, sure. Of course, Larry. I understand. Just, think on it quickly, alright?

LAWRENCE. OK, Donnie. OK. (KATHERINE and WALLY enter. Wally is holding a towel over his eye. KATHERINE seats WALLY in the recliner, drapes the knitted blanket over his shoulders and stands behind the chair comforting WALLY)

DONALD. How's he doing, Kate?

KATHERINE. He's fine.

LAWRENCE. Hey, Wally. How you feeling? (WALLY does not answer)

DONALD. (DONALD, with the sack of quarters in hand, moves to WALLY, kneels beside him between the couch and chair and playfully pokes WALLY in the chest) Quack, quack, like a duck, Wally.

WALLY. (WALLY half-heartedly pokes DONALD back) Quack, quack, like a duck, Donald.

LAWRENCE. (LAWRENCE, separated from the others, remains in the chair at the table) Quack, quack, like a duck, Wally. (WALLY does not respond) Your glasses. Wally, do you want your glassed?

DONALD. Hey, Wally, I cleaned up your quarters.

WALLY. My quarters. Got to make them shiny.

DONALD. You love your shiny quarters, huh, Wally?

WALLY. I love my shiny quarters.

DONALD. (DONALD puts the sack of quarters on the couch out of WALLY's view) You want something real shiny? I have something for you.

WALLY. Yeah.

DONALD. (DONALD takes a small pouch out of his pocket and hands it to WALLY) Wally, this is really expensive, so you have to hold it careful, like it's a baby, alright?

WALLY. (WALLY removes the Silver Dollar from the pouch and holds it up and examines it closely) What's that Donald?

DONALD. It's a silver dollar.

WALLY. That's not a dollar, Donald.

DONALD. It's a silver dollar.

KATHERINE. Wally, look at that. Look at how shiny that silver dollar is. Wow, Wally. I don't have one of those.

WALLY. That's my shiny silver dollar, Kate.

KATHERINE. That is so shiny, Wally.

WALLY. Look, Lawrence. Look at my shiny silver dollar.

LAWRENCE. That's amazing, Wally. You are a special boy.

WALLY. Yeah, Lawrence. That's my shiny silver dollar.

DONALD. Wally, do you know who gave you that silver dollar?

WALLY. Donald.

DONALD. Yes, I gave it to you, but do you know who it's from?

WALLY. Donald?

DONALD. Nope.

WALLY. Daddy?

DONALD. No, Wally. Daddy died.

WALLY. Yeah, Daddy died in a box. I saw him hiding.

DONALD. Wally, this shiny silver dollar is from Mommy.

KATHERINE. What?

DONALD. That's right, Wally. Mommy gave me this shiny silver dollar and she asked me to give it to her special, big boy.

KATHERINE. Are you serious?

DONALD. Yeah.

KATHERINE. You saw her?

DONALD. Yes.

KATHERINE. Where? When?

DONALD. Later, Kate. Wally, did you hear me? Mommy gave me this silver dollar to give to you because she loves you. And she told me to tell you that you don't need to play with your quarters anymore.

WALLY. (WALLY jumps up from the chair and starts looking for Mommy) Mommy!!!!!! Where is she hiding?
DONALD. She's not here, Wally, but do you want to go see her one day?
WALLY. Yeah. (WALLY moves close to LAWRENCE) Mommy gave me a shiny silver dollar.
LAWRENCE. Yes, she did, Wally.
WALLY. Mommy loves me.
LAWERENCE. Yes, she does.
WALLY. Bed time.
LAWRENCE. You tired, Wally?
WALLY. Yeah. Bed time.
LAWRENCE. OK, Wally. Bed time. It's been a long day. Katherine, would you take him upstairs?
WALLY. Donald.
LAWRENCE. You want Donald to put you to bed?
WALLY. Yeah.
DONALD. OK, Wally. Will you show me where your pajamas are?
WALLY. Yeah. Guess what, Donald?
DONALD. What's that, Wally?
WALLY. I can say, "It's bed time" in Latin.
DONALD. In Latin?
WALLY. Yeah. I can say, "It's bed time" in Latin.
DONALD. You can?

WALLY. Yeah. Wanna hear?
DONALD. Sure, Wally.
WALLY. Yeah. A-it's...A-um...A-bed...A-time...A-in...A-Latin. Hahahahaha. I got you, Donald. Let that be a lesson to you.
DONALD. Good one, Wally. That's pig-Latin, right?
WALLY. Yeah. Pig-Latin. Oink, oink like a pig-duck. (WALLY pokes DONALD in the chest) Quack, quack like a duck, Donald. Quack, quack like a duck. Let that be a lesson to you, Donald. Let that be a lesson to you.
DONALD. That's a good lesson, Wally. I like that one, a lot.
KATHERINE. Wally, go on and take Donald up to your room and show him where your pajamas are, ok?
WALLY. Come on, Donald. Bed time. (WALLY takes DONALD's hand and they both begin to exit up to the bedroom. Before they exit, LAWRENCE calls out to DONALD)
LAWRENCE. Donnie.
DONALD. Yeah?
LAWRENCE. You never hit Wally with the bat.
DONALD. No. I never did.
LAWRENCE. OK.
DONALD. OK.
WALLY. Bed time.

DONALD. Come on, Wally. Let's get you into bed.
WALLY. OK, Donald. (DONALD and WALLY exit)
KATHERINE. He found your mother?
LAWRENCE. Yes.
KATHERINE. When?
LAWRENCE. I don't remember what he said.
KATHERINE. Where is she?
LAWRENCE. Providence.
KATHERINE. Oh, my God. What did he say? How is she?
LAWRENCE. She's...I don't want to talk about it right now, Katherine. OK?
KATHERINE. Yes, of course. I'm sorry. You must be exhausted.
LAWRENCE. It's been a long day.
KATHERINE. Can I get you something to eat?
LAWRENCE. Yeah.
KATHERINE. What would you like?
LAWRENCE. It doesn't matter. Anything is fine.
KATHERINE. OK. I'll fix you a plate. (As KATHERINE turns toward the kitchen, WALLY calls from upstairs)
WALLY. Katherine!!! I'm here for you. I'm waiting for you, Katherine. Come tuck me in.
KATHERINE. He called me Katherine.
LAWRENCE. Yes, he did.

KATHERINE. Lawrence...I...

LAWRENCE. It's ok, Kate. Go on. They're waiting for you. (KATHERINE and LAWRENCE stare at each other in silence for a few moments fully realizing the meaning of Donald's return, the revelation of the father's abuse, the discovery that the mother is still alive and the understanding that this is the end of their marriage. KATHERINE exits upstairs. LAWRENCE crosses to the bar behind the couch and pours himself bourbon. He stands in the same position from the start of the play) Let that be a lesson to you, Lawrence. Let that be a lesson to you. (Soft Closing Music fades up as the Lights fade out)

The End

SET

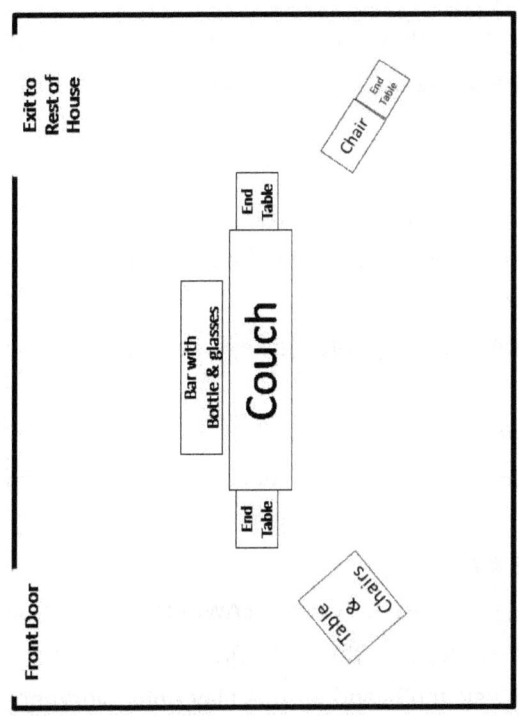

Couch

End Table x 3

Bar Table

Comfortable larger chair

Small Dining Room Table

Chairs or Benches x 2

LIGHTS & SOUND
PRESHOW LIGHTS & SOUND
Mood lights: at 50%

Play audio file 1-PreShow Music.mp3 as people enter the house until the house is full, then pull lights down to black & fade out audio file

SOUND CUE #1
Play audio file 2-CurtainSpeech.mp3 while in blackout
Fade audio file out at the end of the audio clip.

LIGHT CUE #1
As you hear LAWRENCE jingle his keys, raise the lights as he enters

LIGHT CUE #2
As LAWRENCE sits alone on the couch, slowly pull the lights to black

SOUND CUE #2
After the stage is in black, wait for LAWRENCE to exit, and after he is off-stage, play the audio file
3-PostShow Music.mp3 (and let this play until everyone is gone from the theater)

LIGHT CUE #3
Pull lights-up that were set for the entire play, back up for the Curtain Call

LIGHT CUE #4
After the actors exit the stage after the Curtain Call, turn on the house lights

Audio Files can be requested by contacting jared@jaredkelner.com

COSTUMES

DONALD
- Dark jeans, solid long sleeve shirt, old brown leather jacket, sneakers

LAWRENCE
- Traditional funeral black suit, tie, shoes, belt, White shirt (should fit well)

WALLY
- Traditional funeral black suit, tie, shoes, belt, White shirt (should be baggy)
- Grey sweatshirt, Grey sweatpants, White undershirt, White socks, Old slippers

KATHERINE
- Traditional funeral dress or pants outfit, light jacket, shoes, slippers

PROPS

DONALD

- Envelope with Mom's letter inside
- Silver Dollar coin in pouc

LAWRENCE

- House keys
- Watch
- Wallet with 3 $20 dollar bills
- Cellphone
- 3 bottles of alcohol (on the bar)
- 1 glass (on the bar)

WALLY

- Small material bag for the quarters
- 50 quarters
- Reading glasses
- Small towel

KATHERINE

- Black Purse
- Plastic glass of water

GENERAL

- Child's knitted blanket and 2 rag quilts
- Photo album with pictures
- 2 plates, knives, forks, spoons, napkins
- Small garbage can
- 3 Small plants & 4 "Condolence" cards

Silver Dollar
by Jared Kelner

Title: Silver Dollar

Publisher: The Infinite Mind Training Group
(www.memory-trainers.com)

Playwright: Jared Kelner
(www.jaredkelner.com)

ISBN-13: 978-0-9826558-9-4
ISBN-10: 0982655894

All rights reserved. No part of this book may be reproduced or transmitted in any form or by any means without written permission from the playwright, except for the inclusion of brief quotations in a review.

Copyright © 2016 by Jared Kelner
All rights reserved.
First Edition, 2016

Published in the United States of America

Written and Directed
by Jared Kelner

SILVER DOLLAR was produced by Fearless Productions and premiered at The Loft Theater at the Union County Performing Arts Center in Rahway, NJ on 4/8/2016, 4/9/2016 and 4/10/2016.

For Performance Inquiries
Contact Jared Kelner at
jared@jaredkelner.com

To watch a video of the
original cast performance,
please visit
www.jaredkelner.com/Pages/silverdollar.aspx

www.ingramcontent.com/pod-product-compliance
Lightning Source LLC
Chambersburg PA
CBHW071411040426
42444CB00009B/2196